Nutritional aspects of
the development of cancer

A briefing paper prepared for the Health Education Authority.
First draft by Dr Sheila Bingham, subsequent draft by Fiona Wilcock.

Other briefing papers from the HEA

Diet and health in school age children
Dietary fats
Nutritional aspects of cardiovascular
disease
Scientific basis of nutrition education
Sugars in the diet

Health Education Authority
Trevelyan House
30 Great Peter Street
London SW1P 2HW

www.hea.org.uk

Printed in Great Britain
11m 3/99

ISBN 0 7521 1100 0

Contents

Summary

It has been estimated that around one-third of all cancers might be influenced by diet. The Committee on Medical Aspects of Food and Nutrition Policy (COMA) brought together a Working Group to review the evidence on diet and cancer in the UK. This briefing paper has been developed following the publication of the COMA report and provides practical advice to help achieve these recommendations.

The recommendations made by the Working Group were as follows:

- to maintain a healthy body weight within the Body Mass Index (BMI) range 20–25 (see p.56) and not to increase it during adult life;

- to increase intakes of a wide variety of fruits and vegetables;

- to increase intakes of dietary fibre (non-starch polysaccharides) from a variety of food sources;

- for adults, individuals' consumption of red and processed meat should not rise; higher consumers should consider a reduction. As a consequence the population average will fall. It is not recommended that individuals consuming below the current average should reduce their intake*;

- these recommendations should be followed in the context of COMA's wider recommendations for a balanced diet rich in cereals, fruits and vegetables;

- the avoidance of ß-carotene supplements as a means of protecting against cancer;

- the need to exercise caution in the use of high doses of purified supplements of other micronutrients, as they cannot be assumed to be without risk.

---

*The current average consumption is 90g cooked-weight red and processed meats a day, while high consumption is defined as 140g a day.

This briefing paper is intended to help professionals understand the role of diet in the development of cancer. It is organised so that the reader should be able to find information easily. The early sections, 1–5, provide the background to subsequent sections. They highlight the main cancers found in Britain and explain the epidemiology behind the dietary associations. Two main sections (6 and 7) provide details of the links between diet and cancer. In section 6, the main sites of cancer are listed and the dietary associations at each are identified. In 7, the dietary associations, now translated into recommendations, are listed and the cancer sites associated with each are identified. The data can thus be approached by site or by diet. Section 8 provides practical advice on how the dietary recommendations can be implemented using the Balance of Good Health (see p.46) as a basis. The final section, 9, provides information on the report in a simple question and answer format.

1 Introduction

Cancer is the second most common cause of death in Great Britain. About one in three people will develop cancer at some time during their life, and it accounts for about one in four of all deaths. About 160,000 deaths from cancer are registered in Britain each year.

Diet is only one of the environmental and lifestyle factors that are associated with an increased risk of cancer, as shown below. The links between lifestyle factors and cancer risk are very diverse. For some, such as smoking, a causal effect is clear. For others the link is less clear.

Environmental and lifestyle factors associated with an increased risk of cancer:

- Smoking

- Alcohol use

- Diet

- Exposure to chemical hazards

- Exposure to sunlight

- Exposure to ionising radiation

- Exposure to air and water pollutants

- Reproductive and sexual behaviour

- Viral infections.

The Committee on Medical Aspects of Food and Nutrition Policy (COMA) brought together a Working Group to review the evidence on diet and cancer in the UK. This briefing paper provides details of the resulting report *Nutritional Aspects of the Development of Cancer*[1]. It also updates the previous HEA briefing paper on *Diet and Cancer*, published in 1990.

Alcohol was the subject of another Government report[2], and food contaminants and additives are the responsibility of other expert groups[3]. The focus of the COMA report and this briefing paper is the nutritional aspects of the development of cancer. The effects of alcohol are mentioned briefly where there is particular relevance and are based on the *Sensible Drinking* report[2].

Virtually every food or nutrient has been alleged either to cause or protect against cancer, and there are many sites where diet is thought to be important. The Working Group used different types of scientific investigation, mainly concentrated on humans, to make recommendations. The recommendations are made in the expectation that even modest changes to the diet might lower the likelihood that cancers will develop and so prevent many deaths.

WHICH CANCERS WERE INCLUDED IN THE REPORT?

Fifteen major cancers were reviewed by the Working Group. Only those cancers with proposed dietary links are reported in this briefing paper. These include:

- breast cancer

- lung cancer

- colorectal cancer (bowel cancer)

- prostate cancer

- gastric cancer (stomach)

- bladder cancer

- cervical cancer

- ovarian cancer

- endometrial cancer

- pancreatic cancer

- oesophageal cancer

- laryngeal, oral (mouth) and pharyngeal cancer.

Cancer of the skin (melanoma), testis and kidney have not been proposed to have major dietary risk factors associated with them and they are only briefly mentioned. Cancer of the liver was not included in the above review but it was included in the review of alcohol.

2   What is cancer?

Cancer describes a wide variety of growths composed of abnormal disorganised cells. This primary cancer can start to invade neighbouring tissues or spread to distant sites (secondary cancers). Primary cancers can occur in any part of the body, but the major cancers generally occur in epithelial tissues such as the lung, gut or skin. These cancers seem to have the greatest association with lifestyle factors.

Cancers occur when the normal renewal and replacement process of cells goes out of control and the result is abnormal cells. Typically, control is lost over the rate at which cells divide to form new cells and the rate at which they die, so that increased numbers of cells form a tumour, and the cells in the tumour lose their specialised function. It is thought that this occurs as a result of mutations in, or loss of, genes (through damage to DNA), which are then passed to later generations of cells. The changes in the genetic make-up of the cells bring about abnormal functions. An accumulation of genetic changes within the cell and its mutant offspring leads to the formation of a malignant tumour.

The lifestyle or environmental factors (smoking, alcohol, diet, etc.) are thought to be involved in three ways:

- causing the damage to DNA;

- interfering with its repair;

- promoting the growth of damaged cells.

However, how this actually happens is not well understood, especially in relation to diet. Cancers arise because of a complex interaction of genetics, environment and chance.

GENETIC PREDISPOSITION TO CANCER

It is likely that most cancers cannot be explained by known genetic predisposition. This means that the majority of cancers are caused by environmental or lifestyle factors rather than inherited factors.

In the majority of common cancers, affected patients have no family history of cancer, and the genetic damage occurs in the organ where the cancer first arises. However, a minority of cancer patients (between 1% and 5%) have a genetic predisposition to specific cancers. This is because mutant genes were passed on in either the sperm or ova by the parents. These individuals have a high risk of developing the cancer characteristic of the gene mutation type.

GLOBAL GEOGRAPHICAL VARIATION

There is enormous geographical variation in the extent to which particular sites are affected by cancer. In Britain and other developed countries the chances of developing cancer of the lung, large bowel, breast, stomach, prostate and bladder are greater than in less well developed countries. However, cancer of the mouth, cervix and liver are more common in less well developed countries. There are also 'hot spots' of cancers at certain sites in particular geographic regions. For example, oesophageal cancer is common in Iran, and naso-pharyngeal cancer in certain parts of China.

AGE

Common (non-inherited) cancers usually become more prevalent in old age, with a peak between age 65 and 79 in Britain and other developed countries. This is because cancers take years to develop. Lifestyle factors such as smoking, alcohol and diet, which may increase risk, may have been influential decades earlier, possibly in early adulthood or before.

3   Cancer in Britain

Cancer causes one in four deaths (27% in men and 23% in women). Around two-thirds of cancers in the UK are found in 15 body sites. The most common cancers in men are lung, prostate and colorectal cancer, and these account for about 40% of male cancers. In women, breast, colorectal and lung cancer account for 45% of female cancers.

Figures 1a and 1b show the incidence of cancers in men and in women in England, Wales and Scotland.

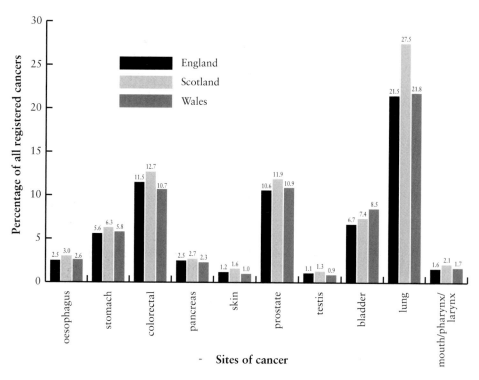

Figure 1a   Relative frequency of cancers at different sites in men (1989)

They show that:

- lung cancer is the most common cancer in men, but is also quite common in women;

- breast cancer is the most common cancer in women;

- colorectal (bowel) cancer is common in men and women;

- cancer of the prostate, stomach and bladder are common in men;

- cancer of the cervix is quite common in women.

Figures 1a and 1b also show that there are geographical differences in cancer incidence.

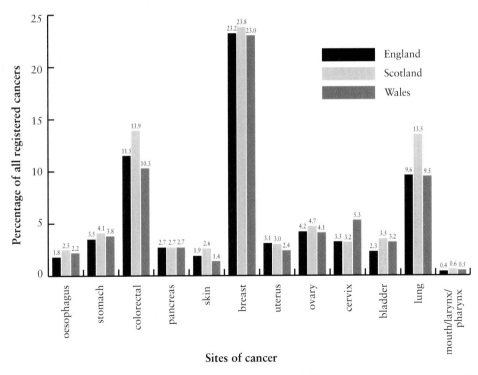

Figure 1b   Relative frequency of cancers at different sites in women (1989)

Strong socio-economic trends exist. People from affluent backgrounds are more likely to have cancer of the breast, colon, prostate, testis, bladder (in men) and skin than are manual and unskilled occupational groups. However, people from manual occupational and unskilled groups are more likely to have cancer of the stomach, oesophagus, rectum (in women), cervix and lung than are those from affluent groups. Overall, the total rate of cancer does not differ.

WHICH CANCERS ARE INCREASING?

Figures 2a and 2b show, over a 15-year period, which cancers are increasing and which are decreasing in Britain.

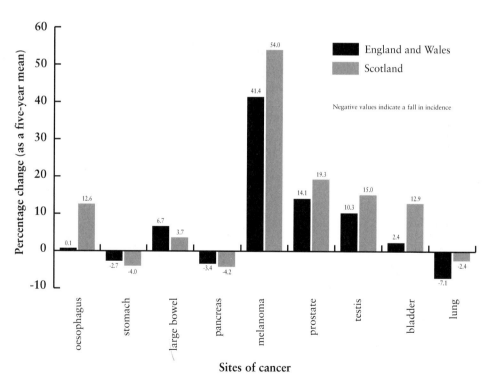

Figure 2a   Changes in incidence of cancers 1973–87 (in 30–74-year-old men)

They show that:

- lung cancer rates are decreasing in men but rapidly increasing in women;

- skin cancer (melanoma) is increasing rapidly in men and women due to increased sun exposure (since diet is not a known risk factor, details are not included in this briefing paper);

- stomach cancer is decreasing in men and women;

- rates of pancreatic cancer are falling in men but rising in women;

- rates of cancer are generally higher in Scotland than in England and Wales.

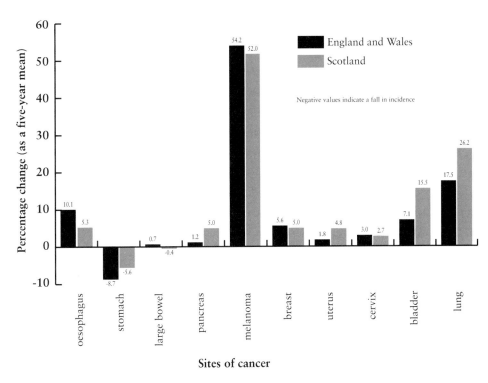

Figure 2b   Changes in incidence of cancers 1973–87 (in 30–74-year-old women)

4 The evidence that relates cancer to diet

The Working Group reviewed epidemiological evidence from case control studies and prospective studies published between 1966 and 1996. This section explains the different types of study that were reviewed.

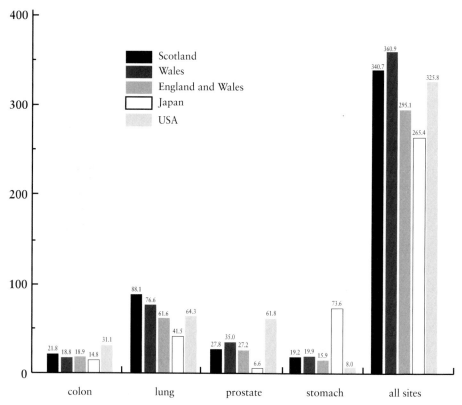

Figure 3a   Age standardised incidence rates for selected cancers (male)

Epidemiology is the study of the distribution and determinants of disease in and between populations. By looking at the characteristics of different populations, it is possible to identify factors that seem to be associated with a higher or lower risk of developing a particular disease. Epidemiological studies do not prove that a factor *causes* a disease but that it is associated with it. Other types of study are needed to prove a mechanism. However, epidemiological studies are important in indicating *possible causes* of disease.

When looking at international data on the incidence of cancer, it is possible to see that the sites of major cancers differ from one country to another. This is shown in Figures 3a and 3b.

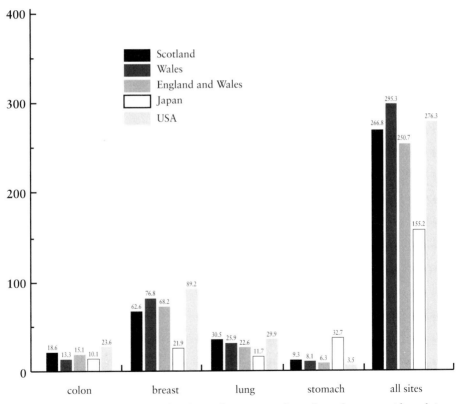

Figure 3b   Age standardised incidence rates for selected cancers (female)

13

World standardised rates of cancer which take age into account show that there are up to 100-fold variations in cancer incidence in different geographical areas. Cancer of the colon is 20 times higher in the USA than in India, and breast cancer is seven times higher in US Hawaiians than in Israeli non-Jews[4].

ARE INHERITED GENETIC FACTORS TO BLAME?

When looking for reasons to explain these huge differences, inherited genetic factors might be thought to play a part. However, three main sources of evidence show that this is not the case.

- Studies of migrants moving from low to high risk areas have shown that the migrants acquire the cancer pattern of the host country within a relatively short period of time. In the case of bowel cancer this could be as short as one generation.

- There are marked trends of cancer incidence with time within countries. For example:

  There is a rising incidence of lung cancer caused by smoking in women in western countries.

  In Japan, bowel cancer rates in men are now higher than those in the UK, whereas only 30 years ago it was virtually unknown.

- Thirdly, some causal links have been established. For example, a clear link is now established between cigarette smoking and lung cancer; tobacco smoke contains known carcinogens.

There are also very strong links between the amount of certain dietary items eaten in various populations and the rates of cancer. Much of the international variation in colorectal cancer can be correlated to dietary differences. **The strength of these associations suggests that a proportion of the variation in cancer incidence is due to differences in dietary practices.**

On the basis of such links, two estimates suggest that, on average, 32–35% of cancers could be prevented by changes in the diet[5, 6]. It is estimated that the contribution of the diet to the incidence of cancer varies from 10% in lung cancer to 80% in colorectal cancer.

DIFFICULTIES IN RELATING DIET AND CANCER

The problem with relating diet to cancer is that the associations are more difficult to detect than for smoking. Whether someone smokes and how many cigarettes he or she smokes are fairly easily quantified. It is known that heavy smokers increase their risk of developing lung cancer by around 50 times.

Substances which cause cancer are known as carcinogens. Some carcinogens induce all stages of cancer development (initiation, promotion and progression), while some are capable only of beginning the sequence. Substances which help prevent cancers developing are generally referred to as anticarcinogens. Components of the diet may be carcinogenic or anticarcinogenic, and some may even be both at different levels of intake or stages of development, which can occur throughout life.

It is less easy to measure dietary components and, even when a link is found, the relative risk of developing a certain cancer rarely increases by more than twofold. This is, in part, due to the methods used, which are unable to distinguish precisely between different aspects of the diet within a population.

METHODOLOGICAL ISSUES

Many studies which have related food to cancer have been carried out by asking patients (cases) who have already developed the disease about their past dietary habits. Their replies are then matched with those from healthy individuals (controls). These **case control studies** may produce biased results because people cannot remember exactly what they used to eat many years ago before they developed cancer. They may also have changed their eating patterns more recently as a result of the disease, or their recollection may be coloured by it.

To help provide more clues about the relationship between diet and cancer, **prospective studies** have been set up. These trials include a very large number of individuals from several populations, so that a wide variety of different dietary habits can be studied for several years before any symptoms of cancer appear. These prospective (also known as cohort) studies also collect biological specimens (blood, urine, etc.)

from the participants. This enables researchers to investigate different types of genes, hormones and damage to DNA as well as markers of diet.

Randomised intervention trials are a definitive way of testing the effect of particular interventions. However, they are not usually applicable:

- to conditions which have a long natural history like many cancers;

- where a large difference between a test and a control group is not expected;

- where large numbers of people need to be involved;

- when prolonged changes in behaviour are involved.

In addition, intervention trials are costly and their value limited because it is not always appropriate to extrapolate the results to other groups.

5   How was the risk of developing cancer assessed?

Various strands of evidence can be used to determine whether diet can cause or prevent cancer. These are summarised in Table 1.

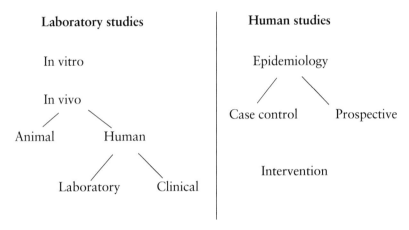

Table 1   The strands of evidence that can be used to determine the effect of diet on cancer

RELATIVE RISK

Relative risk is used to establish how strong the association is between a disease and a risk factor. Relative risks of more than 1.0 indicate an increased likelihood of getting cancer. Relative risks of less than 1.0 mean that the risk of getting cancer is reduced. In common cancers, such as lung, breast and colorectal cancers, even a small reduction in relative risk by reducing smoking or changes in the diet could have a big impact on the numbers of people who develop the disease.

HOW WERE THE RECOMMENDATIONS MADE?

The Working Group used a number of principles to guide them in evaluating the evidence and assessing whether an observed association was likely to be causal. These included:

- the type of study;

- the consistency of results between studies;

- the quality of the studies;

- the size of the relative risk;

- a general tendency for the results to be in the same direction;

- a graded response;

- evidence from randomised controlled trials – this type of evidence is particularly strong evidence for causality;

- evidence of a plausible mechanism;

- timing of exposure and effect.

Recommendations were made where the overall evidence was strong enough and consistent enough to do so. In section 7, the strength of the overall evidence used to make each recommendation is clearly presented in tabular and discursive format.

6 What are the causes of cancer at each of the main sites?

BREAST CANCER

Breast cancer is the most common cancer in women in the UK, affecting over 30,000 women a year. England and Wales have the highest mortality rates from breast cancer in the world, and post-menopausal breast cancer incidence is increasing in the UK. Two of the identified genes account for 4% of breast cancers. Environmental and lifestyle factors, including diet, are therefore the main cause of this increase.

What are the non-dietary risk factors?

These include:

● early menarche*

● late first pregnancy

● few or no children

● late menopause

● hormone replacement therapy (HRT)

● greater height*

● alcohol.

After the menopause the risk of developing breast cancer is associated with higher levels of circulating oestrogens.

Alcohol probably increases the likelihood of developing breast cancer, but the mechanism is not clear. The *Sensible Drinking* report[2] recommends that this association be kept under review.

Risk factors marked with an asterisk(*) may be indirectly related to diet.

What are the dietary risk factors?

Strong evidence	Weak evidence	Inconsistent or insufficient evidence
Obesity, particularly central obesity (post-menopausal only)	Low fruit and vegetable consumption	Low dietary fibre consumption
	High consumption of red and fried meat	Low antioxidant vitamin intake

Summary table of dietary risk factors in breast cancer

Body weight and body fat. Body fat is able to produce oestrogens and after the menopause it provides the main source. Women who are overweight have an increased risk of developing breast cancer post-menopausally, especially if fat is deposited centrally (round the waist). Being overweight does not appear to affect the risk of developing cancer before the menopause. Tall women are also at risk of the disease, but again only after the menopause.

Fat. The role of dietary fat in breast cancer is not clear, but its level of consumption does influence obesity, age of menarche and serum oestrogen levels.

Many studies have looked at the association between breast cancer and fat intakes.

- The rates of breast cancer are lower in populations which eat little fat.

- Most case control studies show that women who develop breast cancer after the menopause report having eaten more fat than women without breast cancer.

- Prospective studies do not show this association of high fat intake and the risk of developing breast cancer.

Several studies have looked at the association between different fatty acids (saturated, monounsaturated, polyunsaturated) and the risk of developing breast cancer. However, the results do not show an association between individual fatty acids and breast cancer.

Fruit and vegetables. High fruit and vegetable consumption is associated with a lower risk of breast cancer.

Meat. Red and fried meat particularly seems to be associated with a higher risk of developing breast cancer. The cause is not clear, but the possibilities might include:

- the formation of heterocyclic amines when meat is cooked (browned) – these are absorbed from the gut and have been shown to cause mammary tumours in animals;

- N-nitroso compounds are formed in the colon after eating meat – these are also known to cause mammary (and colorectal) cancer in rats.

Metabolically active compounds in plants. Chemicals in plants, which are chemically similar to oestrogens, known as phytoestrogens, may influence the process leading to cancer. However, they are in competition with endogenous oestrogens, and the result may be antioestrogenic. Phytoestrogens are found in soya and linseed in large amounts, and in cereal, legumes and vegetables in lower concentrations. There is insufficient evidence from studies to suggest that higher intakes of phytoestrogens will protect against breast cancer.

Antioxidants. Antioxidants such as vitamins C and E, carotenoids and the mineral selenium can prevent oxidation and thus damage to DNA. However, there is insufficient evidence to suggest that an increase would decrease the risk of developing breast cancer for the healthy population.

What are antioxidants?

Antioxidants are molecules which inhibit the oxidation of proteins, lipids and DNA by other molecules called free radicals. It is thought that DNA damage by oxidation is one of the events in cancer development.

The body has a range of defence mechanisms against oxidative damage, including using vitamins C and E, carotenoids and enzymes which rely on selenium, zinc and manganese.

Fruits and vegetables are a major source of antioxidant vitamins.

Early diet. Diet in childhood and adolescence may affect the likelihood of developing breast cancer in later life, because of its effect on the age at which menstruation commences (menarche). Menarche is hastened by high energy (and thus high fat) diets and high meat consumption. Menarche is delayed by higher intakes of grains, nuts and legumes.

LUNG CANCER

Smoking is the most important cause of lung cancer. In Europe and North America, 90% of cases of lung cancer in men and 70–90% of cases in women are estimated to be caused by smoking.

Figure 1a (p.8) shows that lung cancer is the most common cancer in men, though Figure 2a (p.10) also indicates that the disease is declining in men. In women, however, the rate is increasing as the number of female smokers increases (Figure 2b, p.11), and the incidence of lung cancer is second only to breast cancer in women (Figure 1b, p.9).

What are the non-dietary risk factors?

These include:

- smoking

- asbestos

- ionising radiation.

What are the dietary risk factors?

Weak evidence	Inconsistent or insufficient evidence
High meat consumption	Low fruit and vegetable consumption
	Low antioxidant vitamin consumption

Summary table of dietary risk factors in lung cancer

No other risk factors are as strongly associated with the development of lung cancer as smoking.

Meat. There is only a little evidence for an association between high total levels of meat consumption and a higher risk of lung cancer.

Fruits and vegetables. There is some evidence that people who develop lung cancer eat less fruit and vegetables than do healthy controls. However, it is difficult to completely remove the possibility of smoking affecting this association, because smokers are known to eat less fruit and vegetables than do non-smokers.

Vitamins. As a result of early case control studies which suggested that vegetables might suppress lung cancer, it was suggested that the active constituent might be ß-carotene. The antioxidant properties of ß-carotene were thought to protect against damage to DNA. Two recent large intervention trials set up to investigate the benefits of ß-carotene have found that taking high doses of ß-carotene was more harmful than beneficial. Smokers who took the ß-carotene had a higher risk of lung cancer and heart disease compared with people who did not.

Vitamin C and selenium are also antioxidants which might be expected to protect against lung cancer, but the results of studies are inconsistent.

COLORECTAL CANCER

Colorectal cancer is the second most common cancer for men and women in the UK today. Colorectal cancer (also called bowel cancer) refers to cancer in the colon and rectum.

There is a fifteenfold range in the incidence of colorectal cancer throughout the world. Countries with the highest risk include New Zealand, Australia, the USA and parts of northern Europe. Those with the lowest rates include rural Africa, India and China. Populations at low risk of developing colorectal cancer consume little meat and fat, and more plant foods such as vegetables and starchy staples, than do those at high risk. Their intake of dietary fibre (non-starch polysaccharides) is much greater than higher risk populations. Migrants moving from low to high risk areas quickly acquire the incidence rates of the host population.

What are the non-dietary risk factors?

Colorectal cancer has the most well-developed genetic model for its causation. Scientists have established that only 2–4.5% of cases of colorectal cancer are caused by the inherited forms of the diseases (human non-polyposis colon cancer and familial adenomatous polyposis coli).

Physical activity may have a role in reducing colorectal cancer, and although some studies have reported protective effects, others failed to find a relationship. There is no association between alcohol consumption and cancer of the colon. However, there is a weak association between beer consumption and cancer of the rectum.

Known risk factors include:

- sedentary lifestyle;

- adenomatous polyps, ileo-rectal anastomosis and ulcerative colitis;

- mutations to certain genes;

- low stool weight and constipation (though this may arise from diets containing little dietary fibre).

What are the dietary risk factors?

Moderate evidence	Weak evidence	Inconsistent or insufficient evidence
High red and processed meat consumption	High fat consumption	Low antioxidant vitamin (C and E and carotenoids) consumption
Low dietary fibre consumption	Overweight and obesity	
Low vegetable consumption		

Summary table of dietary risk factors in colorectal cancer

Meat. Much of the international variation in colorectal cancer is related to diet, especially meat and fat consumption. Studies show evidence of increased risks of colorectal cancer with red or processed meat consumption, but not with fish or chicken. The highest risk (relative risk of 1.7) was found in people who consumed around two portions of red or processed meat a day, or more.

The link between high intakes of red and processed meat and the increased risk of colorectal cancer could be due to:

- the formation of heterocyclic amines when meat is cooked (browned). These have been found to cause colon cancer when fed in large quantities to animals. It is thought that some humans have different forms of enzymes that break down these heterocyclic amines, which puts them at more risk than others.

- levels of ammonia are increased in the bowel from eating meat. This is thought to increase the risk of developing colorectal cancer.

- N-nitroso compounds (NOC) are formed in the colon after eating meat. High meat consumers are likely to form more NOC, which are regarded as possible carcinogens.

- the iron contained in red meat may act as a pro-oxidant, encouraging damage to DNA.

Dietary fibre. This is supplied by cereals, vegetables and fruit in the diet. Dietary fibre is thought to help regulate bowel function by:

- stimulating fermentation by microbial flora;

- reducing transit time;

- increasing stool bulk.

It is also postulated that the end products of fermentation, especially butyric acid, protect against cell damage by slowing down rates of cell growth. This allows more time for DNA to be repaired, or may stimulate cells to die off, which means they cannot reproduce abnormally.

High stool weight, which is achieved through eating a diet high in cereals, fruits and vegetables, is associated with lower levels of colorectal cancer.

Vegetables. These appear to provide protection against developing colorectal cancer. Vegetarians are at lower risk of colorectal cancer than are meat and fish eaters. High vegetable diets are thought to be protective because of the:

- dietary fibre content;

- antioxidant content;

- presence of other metabolically active compounds;

- lower fat and meat consumption in people who eat more fruit and vegetables.

Fat. There is weakly consistent evidence that diets which are higher in fat are associated with a higher risk of developing colorectal cancer. High fat diets tend to increase the concentration of bile acids in the colon. These are converted to secondary bile acids by the colonic bacteria, and one in particular, deoxycholic acid, increases the rate of cell division in the colon. This might increase the risk of cancer.

Body weight. In men, being overweight may increase the risk of developing colorectal cancer. This association is not seen in women. High activity jobs and high levels of recreational activity are reported to reduce the risk of colorectal cancer, and this is usually attributed to reduced transit time through the gut. However, this might be due to increased starch and dietary fibre consumption due to higher levels of exercise and greater appetite, or to other mechanisms not yet elucidated.

PROSTATE CANCER

Prostate cancer is the third most common cancer in UK men, and its incidence is increasing (see Figure 2a, p.10). Rates of prostate cancer vary throughout the world, and some of the variations are difficult to explain.

What are the non-dietary risk factors?

There is virtually a twofold higher incidence of prostate cancer in blacks than whites in the USA. A history of sexually transmitted disease is a strong indicator of risk in both blacks and whites.

What are the dietary risk factors?

Weak evidence	Inconsistent or insufficient evidence
High total meat consumption	Overweight and obesity
	Low fruit and vegetable consumption
	Low antioxidant vitamin consumption
	High fat consumption

Summary table of dietary risk factors in prostate cancer

Meat. There is weakly consistent evidence and only moderate epidemiological data that red meat consumption is associated with an increased risk of prostate cancer.

Vegetables. In prospective studies, eating large amounts of vegetables, particularly tomatoes and salads, has been associated with a lower risk of developing the disease.

Fruit. Some, but not all, studies show a protective effect of eating fruit.

Fat. In international comparisons of food intake and cancer mortality, high rates of prostate cancer are associated with high fat intake. However, epidemiological studies only provide weak evidence that high fat diets and increased risk of prostate cancer are linked.

STOMACH CANCER

Stomach cancer is the fifth most common cancer in the UK, but in Asian countries such as China and Japan it is one of the most common cancers. Migrant studies suggest that populations moving away from high risk areas keep their high risk of cancer but their children have lower risks. Studies in China point to high salt intakes, and in Japan to intakes of salted fish and pickled vegetables, as major risk factors.

What are the non-dietary risk factors?

The bacteria *Helicobacter pylori* is thought to be the main cause of stomach cancer. Smoking has also been implicated.

What are the dietary risk factors?

Moderate evidence	Inconsistent or insufficient evidence
Low fruit and vegetable consumption	High meat consumption High fat intake Low intakes of antioxidant vitamins

Summary table of dietary risk factors in stomach cancer

Fruits and vegetables. High intakes of fruit and vegetables appear to be protective against stomach cancer.

Vitamins. High intakes of vitamin C (from foods) are strongly associated with a decreased risk of stomach cancer, as are high intakes of carotenoids (ß-carotene and similar compounds), though the evidence is less strong. It is not clear if these are the active substances in fruits and vegetables responsible for their effect.

People who have very low intakes of dietary antioxidants (vitamins C and E, carotenoids and selenium) appear to have a decreased risk of stomach cancer when supplementing their diet with these antioxidants. However, this is not the case for people with intakes in the normal range, and it is not clear which nutrient or combination of nutrients is responsible for the effect.

BLADDER CANCER

Figures 1a and 1b (pp.8, 9) show that bladder cancer is more common in men than women in Britain, although rates are increasing in women (Figure 2b, p.11).

What are the non-dietary risk factors?

These include:

● smoking;

● occupational exposure to organic chemicals;

● infection with bilharzia.

What are the dietary risk factors?

Inconsistent or insufficient evidence

Low fruit and vegetable consumption

Antioxidant vitamin consumption

High meat consumption

Summary table of dietary risk factors in bladder cancer

Since many substances are excreted through the urinary tract, a link between diet and bladder cancer might be expected to exist. However, there have been very few studies to test this.

Fruits and vegetables. There is some evidence that the risk of developing bladder cancer is lower in people who have a higher consumption of fruits and vegetables.

Meat. There have been too few studies to draw conclusions.

CANCER OF THE CERVIX

Cancer of the cervix is the most common cancer in women in developing countries and in Britain is the most common cancer in women aged 20–35, especially those living in Wales.

What are the non-dietary risk factors?

These include:

- infection with human papilloma viruses;
- smoking;
- early age at first intercourse;
- multiple sexual partners.

What are the dietary risk factors?

Insufficient evidence

Low intakes of fruit and vegetables

Low intakes of vitamins A, C and E, and carotenoids

High intakes of meat

High intakes of fat

Summary table of dietary risk factors in cancer of the cervix

Limited information shows that the risk of cancer of the cervix is lower for women who eat greater amounts of fruit and vegetables. This is reinforced by limited evidence showing that higher intakes and/or blood levels of vitamin A, carotenoids, vitamins C and E, and folates (which are found in vegetables and fruit) are associated with a decreased risk.

CANCER OF THE ENDOMETRIUM

Cancer of the endometrium (lining of the womb) is more common in developed countries, with a pattern of hormonal risk factors similar to breast cancer. It is more common in unmarried women and women who have not had children.

What are the non-dietary risk factors?

There are no known non-dietary risk factors.

What are the dietary risk factors?

The most important risk factor is obesity, which is thought to increase the production of oestrogens (also a risk factor for breast cancer).

Strong evidence
Overweight and obesity

Summary table of dietary risk factors in cancer of the endometrium

PANCREATIC CANCER

This disease has a very poor survival rate, 95% of cases dying within five years. There are large international differences in its incidence, with higher rates in developed countries. Rates are increasing in women in Britain and decreasing in men.

What are the non-dietary risk factors?

Smoking accounts for up to 40% of the risk in men and up to 20% in women.

What are the dietary risk factors?

Moderate evidence	Weak evidence	Inconsistent or insufficient evidence
Low dietary fibre consumption	High meat consumption	High fat intakes Low fruit and vegetable consumption Obesity

Summary table of dietary risk factors in pancreatic cancer

Meat. High levels of total and red meat consumption have been found to be associated with an increased risk of pancreatic cancer, but there is only little evidence and no clear mechanism.

Fruits and vegetables. Although there are only a few studies the epidemiological evidence is consistent, showing an association between high intakes of fruit and vegetables and lower rates of pancreatic cancer.

CANCER OF THE OESOPHAGUS

Rates of oesophageal cancer vary throughout the UK, with Scotland having higher rates, particularly in men.

What are the non-dietary risk factors?

In Europe, smoking and alcohol consumption are estimated to account for about 80–90% of oesophageal cancer. There is evidence that alcohol and tobacco interact in a multiplicative fashion.

Alcohol. The risk of developing oesophageal cancer increases by 3–8 times when over 40g of alcohol a day (5 units) is regularly consumed. There is also a risk of developing cancer at 30–40g a day, equivalent to around 4–5 units of alcohol. However, the mechanism of the effect of alcohol on cancer is not understood.

What are the dietary risk factors?

Inconsistent or insufficient evidence
Low antioxidant vitamin intake
High meat consumption
Low fruit and vegetable intake
High intake of fat

Summary table of dietary risk factors in oesophageal cancer

Antioxidant vitamins. Higher levels of antioxidant vitamins from food are associated with a lower risk of developing the disease. However, when intervention trials have been used, there has been no reduction of risk.

Fruits and vegetables. Studies of populations outside the UK show that people with high intakes of fruit and vegetables are less likely to develop oesophageal cancer. Studies in the UK are limited.

CANCER OF THE MOUTH, LARYNX AND PHARYNX

Mouth and pharynx cancers account for about 6% of cancer worldwide and are more common in developing countries than in developed ones. This group of cancers varies by region, with mouth and tongue cancer being the most common in India (related to betel nut chewing), and naso-pharyngeal cancer in south-east Asia and China (related to salt fish consumption). In Britain, cancer of the larynx is the most common of these cancers, especially in men. The incidence is higher in Scotland than in England and Wales (see Figures 1a and 1b, pp.8, 9), although it is still comparatively rare compared with cancers described earlier.

What are the non-dietary risk factors?

Smoking is a major risk factor. In addition, although smoking and alcohol cause these cancers independently, each compounds the effect of the other.

What are the dietary risk factors?

Inconsistent or insufficient evidence

High meat consumption

Summary table of dietary risk factors in cancers of the mouth, larynx and pharynx

Vegetables. Along with fruits, vegetables are thought to be protective against laryngeal cancer, though this effect is minimal compared with the effects of smoking and alcohol.

Fruits. These appear to be protective for all three of these cancers.

CANCER AT OTHER SITES – LIVER, SKIN, TESTIS, OVARY AND KIDNEY

Food does not appear to be a major risk factor for these cancers. Heavy alcohol consumption is known to be a major contributory factor for liver cancer.

Liver cancer

What are the non-dietary risk factors?

- Alcohol consumption

- Hepatitis B infection

- Aflatoxin infection.

What are the dietary risk factors?

There do not appear to be any dietary risk factors associated with cancer at this site.

Skin cancer

What are the non-dietary risk factors?

- Sunlight exposure.

What are the dietary risk factors?

There is inconclusive evidence of an inverse risk of skin cancer with vitamin E intake.

Testicular cancer

What are the non-dietary risk factors?

- Undescended testis.

What are the dietary risk factors?

High consumption of fat and dairy products has been suggested as a possible dietary risk factor, but there is insufficient evidence to support this.

Ovarian cancer

What are the non-dietary risk factors?

- Late menopause
- Infertility
- Possession of certain genes.

What are the dietary risk factors?

Low vegetable consumption and high intakes of fat, dairy products and meat have been explored as possible dietary risk factors, but there is insufficient evidence of an association.

Kidney cancer

What are the non-dietary risk factors?

- Smoking.

What are the dietary risk factors?

There do not appear to be any dietary risk factors associated with cancer at this site.

7 What are the dietary recommendations and why have they been made?

This section looks at each of the dietary recommendations, briefly explaining the evidence behind the recommendation and discussing plausible mechanisms where they exist. The various sites of cancer associated with the dietary component are shown, together with the strength of the evidence used to make the recommendation. This section also provides the recommendations on alcohol. The following section (8) provides practical suggestions for implementing the recommendations.

DIETARY RECOMMENDATIONS

The recommendations are:

- to maintain a healthy body weight within the BMI range 20–25 (see p.56) and not to increase it during adult life;

- to increase intakes of a wide variety of fruits and vegetables;

- to increase intakes of dietary fibre (non-starch polysaccharides) from a variety of food sources;

- for adults, individuals' consumption of red and processed meat should not rise; higher consumers should consider a reduction*. It is not recommended that individuals consuming below the current average should reduce their intake;

---

*The current average consumption is 90g cooked-weight red and processed meats a day, while high consumption is defined as 140g a day.

- these recommendations should be followed in the context of COMA's wider recommendations for a healthy, balanced and varied diet, in particular one rich in cereals, fruit and vegetables;

- the avoidance of ß-carotene supplements as a means of protecting against cancer;

- the need to exercise caution in the use of high doses of purified supplements of other micronutrients as they cannot be assumed to be without risk.

Through the implementation of these recommendations, even a small reduction in relative risk for the major cancers could represent the saving of many thousands of lives.

The recommendations also reinforce, and are consistent with, other dietary recommendations made for the avoidance of obesity, diabetes and cardiovascular disease. These have been translated into practical messages through the Balance of Good Health, which is explained in section 8.

The recommendations are intended for all adults and children aged over 5 years, unless medically advised to the contrary.

Alcohol was the subject of a separate report. It has a multiplicative effect with smoking on certain cancers, and high levels of alcohol consumption, especially with smoking, increase the risk of cancer of the liver, mouth (oral cavity), larynx, pharynx and oesophagus. **The recommended benchmark for men is to drink no more than between 3 and 4 units a day. For women the recommended benchmark is to drink no more than between 2 and 3 units a day.**

Recommendation: to maintain a healthy body weight within the BMI range 20–25 and not to increase it during adult life.

Obesity is strongly associated with an increased risk of post-menopausal breast cancer and endometrial cancer in women. The table below shows the strength of the evidence which was used to make the recommendation to maintain a healthy body weight.

Types of cancer	Strength of evidence
Post-menopausal breast cancer and endometrial cancer	Strong evidence
Colorectal cancer	Weak evidence
Prostate, ovarian, pancreatic and testicular cancer	Inconsistent or insufficient evidence

> **Recommendation: to increase intakes of a wide variety of fruits and vegetables.**

High fruit and vegetable consumption is associated with a decreased risk of cancer at many sites. The table below shows the strength of the evidence which was used to make the recommendation to increase fruit and vegetable consumption.

Types of cancer	Strength of evidence
Colorectal and stomach cancer	Moderate evidence
Breast cancer	Weak evidence
Lung, ovarian and oesophageal cancer	Insufficient evidence
Prostate, cervical, pancreatic and bladder cancer	Few studies, but all are moderately or strongly consistent

Increased consumption of vegetables appears to confer a protective effect against **colorectal** cancer, whilst fruit and vegetable consumption appears to be protective against **stomach** cancer. Vegetarians are reported to have a lower risk of developing colorectal cancer, and studies indicate that this is due to greater levels of vegetable consumption.

There is no evidence that eating more fruits or vegetables increases the risk of developing cancer. Moreover, there is some evidence that the more fruit and vegetables eaten, the more protection is provided.

In populations, for example those in Mediterranean regions, where more than twice the amount of fruits and vegetables is regularly eaten than in Britain, cancer rates are considerably lower, which is consistent with a strong protective effect of fruit and vegetables. Doubling the UK consumption to at least five portions of fruits and vegetables a day would be expected to provide protection against colorectal and stomach cancer in particular, and to provide other health benefits too. Examples of how this can be achieved are found in section 8.

Fruits and vegetables are composed of many components, including starches and sugars, protein, vitamins including important antioxidants and folates, minerals, dietary fibre and metabolically active compounds. This latter group includes carotenoids, flavonoids and sulphur-containing compounds, and it is thought that these may be important in reducing the risk of developing cancer. Studies do not show accurately if any one of these factors is more protective than another. However, an overall increase in the amount of fruit and vegetables eaten would lead to increased intakes of folates, antioxidant nutrients, dietary fibre and metabolically active compounds, and might lead to a decrease in meat and fat consumption. Selecting from a wide range of fruits and vegetables would provide a greater variety of micronutrients and other substances than restricting the range to one or two varieties.

> **Recommendation: to increase intakes of dietary fibre (non-starch polysaccharides) from a variety of food sources.**

The table below shows the strength of the evidence which was used to make the recommendation.

Types of cancer	Strength of evidence
Colorectal cancer and pancreatic cancer	Moderate evidence
Breast cancer and other cancers	Insufficient or inconsistent evidence

There is moderately good evidence that dietary fibre in foods is important in preventing **colorectal cancer**. Studies show lower risks of developing colorectal cancer with higher intakes of dietary fibre. It is uncertain whether this is due to the overall protective effects of eating a diet high in plant foods and low in meat and fat, or a protective aspect of dietary fibre, such as fermentation in the gut. Increased consumption of dietary fibre has also been found to reduce **pancreatic cancer.**

Several studies have looked at the link between **breast cancer** and dietary fibre, but the evidence is inconsistent. There are plausible reasons why dietary fibre might confer protection, since diets high in dietary fibre lead to a reduction in oestrogens, one of the risk factors for breast cancer. However, it is difficult to determine whether it is dietary fibre *per se* or a lower fat diet with concomitant weight loss which is providing protection.

Support for a causal role of dietary fibre in protecting against colorectal cancer comes from the knowledge that it is important in regulating bowel function, due to its effects on the bacteria of the large bowel. Dietary fibre entering the bowel stimulates fermentation by the bacteria, which increases their mass. This leads to a faster transit time through the gut, increased stool weight (due to dietary fibre and additional bacterial mass) and a dilution of the contents of the colon. Low stool weight leads to constipation, which is known to be a risk factor for bowel cancer.

Dietary fibre may also provide protection via the by-products formed during fermentation. Butyric acid is one by-product which is known to slow the rate at which cells divide, and thus allow more time for the repair of damaged DNA in cells. It also stimulates cells to die off. This provides protection, since the dead cells cannot reproduce and repaired cells behave normally, thus preventing damaged cells progressing to malignancy.

How much dietary fibre is recommended?

The Working Group endorses a previous recommendation by the COMA Panel on Dietary Reference Values of an increase in the amount of dietary fibre consumed from 12g a day to 18g a day. Section 8 provides examples of how the recommendations can be achieved.

> Recommendation: for adults, individuals' consumption of red and processed meat should not rise; higher consumers should consider a reduction; and as a consequence of this the population average will fall. Adults with intakes of red and processed meats greater than the current average, especially those in the upper reaches of the distribution of intakes where the scientific data are more robust, might benefit from and should consider a reduction in intake. It is not recommended that adults with intakes below the current average should reduce their intakes.

The table below shows the strength of the evidence for different cancers which prompted the Working Group to make the recommendation. Red meat refers to beef, pork and lamb. Processed meat includes sausages, hamburgers, cured and salted meat, and canned meats.

Types of cancer	Strength of evidence
Colorectal cancer	Moderate evidence
Breast, lung, prostate and pancreatic cancer	Weak evidence
Bladder, stomach, cervical, ovarian, oesophageal, laryngeal, mouth, pharyngeal and testicular cancer	Inconsistent or insufficient evidence

Colorectal cancer accounts for 12% of all cancers. High levels of consumption of red and processed meat are associated with a higher risk of colorectal cancer. The data seem to point more consistently to red and processed meat rather than other meats. There does not appear to be an association with poultry and fish. Prospective studies show that the risk of developing colorectal cancer may almost double in *high consumers* of red and processed meats. (High consumers is taken to mean people eating 12–14 portions a week averaging 140g or more cooked weight of red and processed meats per day.)

Cooked meats are a source of heterocyclic amines which have been proposed to increase the risk of **colon cancer**, though their importance in humans is uncertain. Nitrogenous residues from meat and other protein-containing foods which enter the large bowel are fermented by bacteria with the production of ammonia. Ammonia increases cell growth and can promote premalignant polyps. In addition, carcinogenic N-nitroso compounds (NOC) are formed in the colon from meat residues, and the formation of these is increased with consumption of red meat, but not white meat or fish.

There is weak evidence that **breast, lung, prostate and pancreatic cancer** are associated with high intakes of red or processed meats. The carcinogenic effect of heterocyclic amines and NOC on these sites in humans has not been studied, but they are known to be absorbed from the human gut and are established mammary carcinogens in rodent models.

> **These recommendations should be followed in the context of COMA's wider recommendations for a healthy, balanced and varied diet, in particular one rich in cereals, fruit and vegetables.**

The Balance of Good Health is a dietary model, which illustrates a varied diet rich in cereals, fruit and vegetables. It is detailed on page 46.

> **The Working Group made no specific recommendations on fat intake.**

Although many studies have looked at the relationship of dietary fat to different cancers, for none is the relationship so strong that the Working Group considered a specific recommendation.

The table below shows the strength of evidence on which the Working Group based its decision not to make a specific recommendation on fat.

Types of cancer	Strength of evidence
Colorectal cancer	Weak evidence (not statistically significant)
Breast cancer	Inconsistent evidence
Prostate, lung, stomach, cervical, oesophageal and pancreatic cancer	Insufficient evidence

There is weakly consistent evidence supported by plausible, but not proven, mechanisms that high fat intakes increase the risk of **colorectal cancer**.

Low fat diets have not been consistently shown to reduce free oestrogens, a risk factor for **breast cancer**. It is postulated that high fat intakes in childhood may hasten menarche and affect the risk of **breast cancer** decades later.

Current dietary advice to reduce the proportion of energy from fat would not be expected to influence the risk of cancer, though it might reduce the likelihood of obesity.

> **Recommendation: the avoidance of ß-carotene supplements as a means of protecting against cancer; the need to exercise caution in the use of high doses of purified supplements of other micronutrients, as they cannot be assumed to be without risk.**

The table below shows the strength of the evidence which prompted the Working Group to recommend the avoidance of ß-carotene supplements.

Types of cancer	Strength of evidence
Lung cancer	Moderate evidence of increased risk in smokers
Breast, colorectal, prostate, stomach, cervical, oesophageal cancers	Insufficient evidence of any effect

Higher dietary intakes of the antioxidant vitamins, carotenoids, vitamin C and vitamin E (from foods) have been associated with reduced risk of developing breast cancer, colorectal cancer, lung cancer, stomach cancer, oesophageal cancer and cervical cancer. It has been suggested that damage to DNA might be prevented by dietary antioxidants. However, when intervention trials have boosted intakes by supplementing with these vitamins, there has been no clear protective effect. There are two possible reasons for this.

- The trials are too short to show a protective effect when compared with the long-term development of the disease.

- Other substances may also be consumed in association with vitamins, when derived from foods, which are not present in vitamin supplements.

Two major studies investigating lung cancer which used supplements of ß-carotene had the unexpected result that the incidence of lung cancer and coronary heart disease rose in those taking the supplements. The exact mechanism is uncertain, but it is possible that using high doses of purified vitamins may adversely affect the balance and functioning of carotenoids in the body. This highlights the need for caution in taking high doses of purified vitamins and minerals in supplement form.

Higher intakes of vitamins can be obtained by increasing consumption of fruit and vegetables.

RECOMMENDATIONS ON ALCOHOL

Alcohol was the subject of the *Sensible Drinking* report[2] from the Department of Health Interdepartmental Working Group, from which the following recommendations are taken.

> **The recommended benchmark for men is to drink no more than between 3 and 4 units a day. For women, the recommended benchmark is to drink no more than between 2 and 3 units a day.**

The Sensible Drinking Message also states that consistently drinking over this amount increases the risk to health. It is particularly important to avoid getting drunk.

Light to moderate drinking – between one and two units of alcohol a day – has a beneficial effect for coronary heart disease for those at risk. This includes men over 40 and women who have been through the menopause.

The Committee on Carcinogenicity (COC) 1996 report[3] cited evidence that moderate to heavy alcohol consumption is linked to cancers of the head and neck, but it was difficult to quantify the risk when compared with non-drinkers or light drinkers. The findings were independent of the effect of smoking. The main sites are the oral cavity (mouth), pharynx, larynx and oesophagus. The COC report cited that the association between alcohol and breast cancer was unclear and should be kept under review.

Type of cancer	Amount of alcohol drunk (g/day)	Units of alcohol	Risk of developing cancer
Mouth	20g and less	2½	Possibility of increased risk
	40g	5	Increased risk
	70–100g	9–12½	8–15 times the risk
Pharynx	20g and less	2½	Possibility of increased risk
	40g	5	Increased risk
	80g and over	10+	5–12 times the risk
Larynx	20g and less	2½	Possibility of increased risk
	40–70g	5–9	Increased risk
	70–100g	9–12½	3–9 times the risk
Oesophagus	30–40g	4–5	Some risk
	40g and over	5	3–8 times the risk

(1 unit of alcohol is equivalent to 8g alcohol. See section 8 for details.)

Table 2   The risk of developing cancer at the main sites in relation to the level of alcohol consumption

8 How can the recommendations be implemented?

This section provides details of how to put the recommendations into practice.

A diet which is high in fruits and vegetables, and contains plenty of starchy foods and only moderate amounts of meat, fish and dairy products is likely to provide protection against cancers and other diet-related diseases. This type of diet is typified by the **Balance of Good Health,** a model produced jointly by the Department of Health, the Ministry of Agriculture, Fisheries and Food and the Health Education Authority in 1996. This model (as shown below) illustrates the desirable balance of foods in the diet for the promotion of good health.

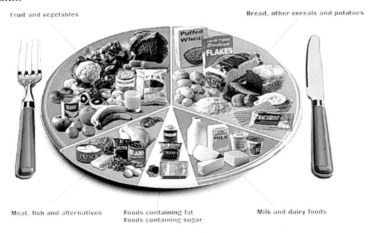

Fruit and vegetables   Bread, other cereals and potatoes

Meat, fish and alternatives   Foods containing fat
Foods containing sugar   Milk and dairy foods

Figure 4   The Balance of Good Health plate

The Balance of Good Health is consistent with the dietary recommendations on cancer and stresses the importance of a balance of different foods and the need for variety.

Food groups	Bread, other cereals and potatoes	Fruits and vegetables	Milk and dairy foods	Meat, fish and alternatives	Foods containing fat; foods containing sugar
What is included	• Bread, rolls, chapattis. • Breakfast cereals, oats. • Pasta, noodles, rice. • Potatoes, sweet potatoes. • Maize, millet. • Plantains, yams, green bananas. • Beans, lentils.	• All fresh, frozen, canned fruit and vegetables. • Salad vegetables. • Beans and lentils. • Fruit juice, dried fruit.	• Milks, cheeses, fromage frais, yogurt.	• Meat – beef, pork, lamb, bacon. • Meat products – sausages, beefburgers. • Liver, kidney. • Chicken, turkey. • Fish and fish products. • Eggs. • Beans and lentils, nuts, textured vegetable protein, other meat alternatives.	• Butter, margarine, low fat spreads, cooking oils. • Mayonnaise and oily salad dressings. • Biscuits, cakes and puddings, ice cream. • Chocolate and sweets. • Crisps and savoury snacks. • Sugar, sweetened drinks.
Recomm-endations	• Eat lots. These foods should make up one-third of the diet.	• Eat at least five portions a day. These foods should make up one-third of the diet.	• Eat or drink moderate amounts.	• Eat moderate amounts of all foods in this group.	• Use fats and oils sparingly. Don't eat the other types of food too often.

Table 3 continued on next page

Table 3 continued

Food groups	Bread, other cereals and potatoes	Fruits and vegetables	Milk and dairy foods	Meat, fish and alternatives	Foods containing fat; foods containing sugar
Recommendations – *continued*	• Choose wholegrain varieties when possible. These foods are the major source of starchy carbohydrate and dietary fibre, especially if wholegrain versions are selected. • Starchy foods are filling and are useful in displacing foods containing fat and foods containing sugar from the diet.	• Fruits and vegetables are a major source of vitamins, minerals and dietary fibre.	• Use lower fat products when possible.	• High consumers of red and processed meat (140g cooked weight and more a day) should cut down. Moderate consumers (90g cooked weight a day) should not increase their consumption of red and processed meat. • Choose lean meat, remove fat, skin poultry. • Eat fish, including oily fish, twice a week. • Include beans and lentils – they contain dietary fibre.	• Use lower fat versions of these foods when possible. • Limit consumption of cakes, biscuits, crisps, confectionery, etc.

Table 3 Shows how the recommendations can be implemented, by food group

The specific recommendations relating to cancer are addressed below.

HOW MUCH FRUIT AND VEGETABLES ARE NEEDED?

The target of doubling fruit and vegetable consumption, recommended in the report on *Nutritional Aspects of Cardiovascular Disease*[7], to at least five portions a day is still not reached by the majority of the population. The report on *Nutritional Aspects of the Development of Cancer*[1] reinforces this recommendation in the light of the association of certain sites of cancer with vegetable and fruit consumption.

Not all fruits and vegetables contain the same mix of vitamins, minerals and metabolically active compounds. For example, yellow and orange fruits and vegetables and dark green vegetables are a good source of carotenoids, whilst kiwi fruit, strawberries and citrus fruits contain large quantities of vitamin C. By eating a wide variety of fruit and vegetables there is a greater likelihood of obtaining beneficial components from them all.

What is a portion of fruit or vegetables?

The five portions of fruit and vegetables a day recommended exclude potatoes and nuts but include beans, peas or lentils. Fresh, frozen, canned and dried fruit and vegetables all count. One or more glasses of fruit juice also counts as one portion.

An average portion of fruit would include:

- 1 slice of very large fruit, e.g. melon, pineapple, papaya;

- ½ avocado or grapefruit;

- 1 large fruit, e.g. apple, pear, banana, large clementine or satsuma, orange, peach, nectarine;

- 2 medium fruit, e.g. apricot, kiwi, plum, small clementine or tangerine;

- 5 small fruit, e.g. damson, lychee, passion fruit;

- 1 cupful of very small fruit, e.g. blackberries, strawberries, raspberries, cherries, grapes;

- 2–3 tablespoons of stewed fruit, canned fruit or fruit salad;

- ½–1 tablespoon of dried fruit, e.g. raisins, apricots, dates, figs;

- 1 or more glasses of fruit juice (150ml).

An average portion of vegetables would include:

- 2 tablespoons of green vegetables, e.g. broccoli, broad beans, courgettes, cauliflower, spinach, leek, cabbage;

- 2 tablespoons of root vegetables, e.g. carrots, parsnips, swede, turnip;

- 2 tablespoons of very small vegetables, e.g. peas, sweetcorn, ratatouille;

- 2 tablespoons of other vegetables, e.g. aubergine, marrow, mushrooms, onion, canned tomatoes;

- 2 tablespoons of beans and pulses, e.g. baked beans, chick peas, lentils, kidney beans;

- 1 bowlful of salad, e.g. cherry tomatoes, lettuce, avocado, cucumber, beetroot, beansprouts.

HOW MUCH DIETARY FIBRE IS NEEDED?

The Working Group endorses a previous recommendation by the COMA Panel on Dietary Reference Values[8] of an increase in the amount of dietary fibre (non-starch polysaccharides) consumed from 12g a day to 18g a day.

National Food Survey data indicate that intakes of dietary fibre have been falling slightly since 1985. The average amount consumed in 1995 was just under 12g a day. Fruit and vegetables contributed 51% of this, and 45% was derived from cereal products such as bread, breakfast cereals, etc.

Good sources of dietary fibre

These include:

- wholegrain cereals – brown rice, wholewheat pasta, wholemeal bread;
- wholegrain or bran-enriched breakfast cereals – muesli, bran flakes, etc.;
- beans, peas and lentils;
- fruit — fresh, frozen, canned or dried;
- vegetables – fresh, frozen or canned.

How is 18g dietary fibre a day achieved?

Table 4 below indicates the amount of dietary fibre contained in some average portions of commonly eaten foods.

Food	Amount of dietary fibre (g)	Weight of portion of food (g)
Cereals		
All Bran	9.8	40
Fibre 1 breakfast cereal	9.2	30
Muesli	3.8	50
Cornflakes	0.3	30
Weetabix	1.9	20
Rice, white, boiled	0.3	150
Wholemeal spaghetti	7.7	220
Wholemeal bread	2.2	38
White bread, sliced	0.5	36
Pitta bread, white	1.6	75
Pulses		
Lentil dhal	4.2	210
Baked beans	5.1	135
Kidney beans	3.7	60

Table 4 continued on next page

Table 4 continued

Food	Amount of dietary fibre (g)	Weight of portion of food (g)
Vegetables		
Sweet potato, baked	4.3	130
Carrots, boiled	1.5	60
Baked potato with skin	4.9	180
Peas, frozen	3.5	70
Sweetcorn	1.9	85
Cabbage	2.6	95
Broccoli	2.0	90
New potatoes in skins	2.6	175
Tomato, raw	0.9	85
Fruits		
Baked apple, no skin	3.2	190
Apricots, dried, ready to eat	2.5	40
Oranges	2.7	160
Fruit salad	2.1	140
Apple, e.g. Cox	2.0	100
Kiwi fruit	1.4	60
Banana	1.1	100
Plums, raw	1.0	55
Pears	4.1	170
Blackcurrants, stewed	4.3	140
Other foods		
Potato crisps	1.6	30
Digestive biscuit	0.3	15

Table 4   Shows how 18g dietary fibre a day can be achieved

HOW CAN THE RECOMMENDED LEVELS FOR FRUITS AND VEGETABLES AND DIETARY FIBRE BE REACHED?

Food	Fibre content (g)	Number of portions of fruit and vegetables
1 glass orange juice	0.0	1
1 bowl cornflakes	0.3	0
1 banana	1.1	1
1 baked potato (medium)	4.9	0
with cheese	0.0	0
and baked beans	5.1	1
1 apple	2.0	1
1 portion lasagne	2.8	0
2 tablespoons carrots	1.5	1
1 chunk of French bread	0.6	0
Total	*18.3*	*5*
Recommendations	*18.0*	*5*

Table 5 An example of how the recommendations for fruit and vegetables and dietary fibre can be met (does not contain all the foods which would be eaten during a day)

WHAT DO THE RECOMMENDATIONS FOR RED AND PROCESSED MEAT MEAN?

COMA suggests that for adults, individuals' consumption of red and processed meat should not rise; higher consumers should consider a reduction: as a consequence of this the population average will fall. Adults with intakes of red and processed meats greater than the current average, especially those in the upper reaches of the distribution of intakes where the scientific data are more robust, might benefit from and should consider a reduction in intake. It is not recommended that adults with intakes below the current average should reduce their intakes.

Red meat refers to beef, pork and lamb. Processed meat refers to sausages, hamburgers, meat pies and pasties, cured and salted meat, such as bacon and ham, and canned meats.

These recommendations should be followed in the context of COMA's wider recommendations for a balanced diet rich in cereals, fruits and vegetables (i.e. one which is consistent with the Balance of Good Health) see p.46. Red and processed meats are part of a wider group of protein-containing foods, and fish, chicken, lentils, beans and other alternatives should also form part of a balanced diet.

Meat is a valuable source of several nutrients in the diet, including protein, vitamin B12, and the minerals iron, zinc and magnesium. Red meat is an especially important source of easily absorbed (haem) iron. Iron status is low in several groups, including some infants, toddlers, adolescents, women in their reproductive years and older people[9]. These individuals need to be encouraged to eat a wide range of sources of iron, including some red meat.

For this reason the recommendation for red and processed meats only applies to *adults* who consume more than the average daily intake of 90g per day of cooked red and processed meat, and especially those with daily intakes of 140g or more (12–14 portions a week) of cooked red and processed meat.

How much cooked red and processed meat is recommended?

Most people who eat meat also eat chicken, fish or alternatives on some days, so that over a period of days the consumption of red and processed meat is rarely high. The average amount of red and processed meat which people eat is therefore calculated over a period of time rather than each day, but this averages out at 90g cooked weight per day.

People with current intakes below the average of 90g per day cooked red and processed meats should not reduce the amount of red and processed meat eaten. People who eat more than this every day should consider eating less, especially those who eat 140g or more per day of cooked red and processed meats. In practical terms this means that on some days a person may eat a cooked portion larger than 90g, and on other days may choose to eat a small amount or no red or processed meat. COMA does not recommend eating more than 90g cooked weight of red and processed meats daily on average.

Most people buy raw meat, and there is a variable amount of weight loss due to cooking and trimming. The following table provides examples of meat portions that weigh approximately either 90g or 140g when cooked.

Examples of approximately 90g portions of cooked meat	Examples of approximately 140g portions of cooked meat
• 1 portion (about 3 slices) of roast beef, lamb or pork	• 2 rashers of back bacon or 2 slices of ham in a salad or sandwich *plus* 1 portion (about 3 slices) of roast beef, lamb or pork
• 1 small portion of meat sauce on pasta	
• 2 rashers of back bacon plus 1 large sausage	• 1 sausage and 2 rashers of back bacon *plus* 1 individual, (or 1 portion of) steak and kidney pie
• 2 standard beefburgers and 1 slice of streaky bacon	
• 1 lamb chump chop	• 4 standard beefburgers
• 1 pork rib end chop	• 3–4 sausages
• 1 lean pork escalope	• 2 large lamb cutlets or 2 average lamb or pork chops
• 1 average beef minute steak	
	• 1 raw-weight steak 6–7oz (170–200g)
	• 1 sausage and 1 rasher of bacon *plus* 1 portion of spaghetti bolognese, lasagne, moussaka or shepherds pie
	• 1 individual pork pie *plus* 1 quarter-pound burger

Table 6   Examples of 90g or 140g meat portions

WHAT IS A HEALTHY BODY WEIGHT?

The usual measure of overweight is called Body Mass Index or BMI. It is calculated by dividing weight in kilograms by height in metres squared.

$$\text{BMI} = \frac{\text{body weight (kg)}}{\text{height (m)}^2}$$

A healthy body weight is having a BMI between 20 and 25.

Having a BMI between 25 and 30 is regarded as being overweight.

Having a BMI of 30 and over is regarded as being obese.

It is not healthy to be underweight or overweight. Keeping within the OK range on the chart will help sustain good health.

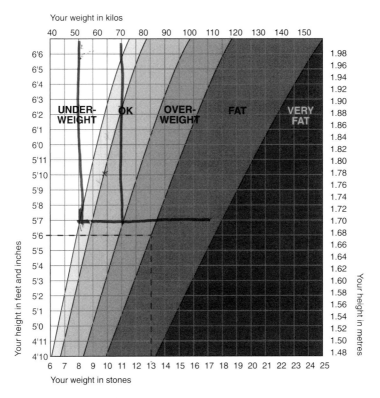

Figure 5 Height/weight chart

How is a healthy body weight maintained?

The most effective way of maintaining a healthy body weight is by being physically active and eating a diet rich in fruit, vegetables and starchy foods, and not much fat. The Health Education Authority's Active for Life[10] campaign recommends that 30 minutes of moderate activity should be taken on at least five days of the week.

What is moderate activity?

Moderate activity is:

- walking briskly
- swimming
- cycling
- gardening
- dancing
- pushing a pram
- low impact aerobics.

This level of exercise should not feel uncomfortable and should be pain free.

Adults who try to maintain their weight through diet alone are much less successful in doing so than adults who increase their physical activity levels in conjunction with eating a healthy diet.

Although **no specific recommendations were made by this Working Group with regard to fat intake**, the COMA Working Group on Nutritional Aspects of Cardiovascular Disease made recommendations which should still be followed. These were a reduction in the average amount of food energy provided by fat for the population to 35% and an increase in oily fish consumption. For example, oily fish such as mackerel, herring, sardine, trout, salmon and pilchard are recommended to be eaten at least once a week.

Current recommendations to decrease the proportion of energy derived from fat in the diet might reduce the likelihood of obesity. Since this is a risk factor in several cancers (breast and endometrial cancer in women, and colorectal cancer in men), a reduction in fat intake may indirectly affect the risk of developing cancer. Eating a diet consistent with the Balance of Good Health (see p.46), which is high in starchy foods, fruit and vegetables, helps displace more fatty foods.

Although **no specific recommendations were made by this Working Group on alcohol consumption**, alcohol was the subject of another Government report[2]. The Sensible Drinking Message derived from the

Department of Health Inter-departmental Working Group suggested that the recommended benchmark for men is to drink no more than between 3 and 4 units a day. For women, the recommended benchmark is to drink no more than between 2 and 3 units a day.

What is a unit of alcohol?

One unit of alcohol is 8 grams. This is the amount contained in:

- half a pint of ordinary beer or lager (284ml);

- 2 pints of low alcohol beer or cider (1.1l);

- quarter of a pint of strong lager, beer or cider (142ml);

- a small glass of wine (100ml);

- a small glass of sherry or fortified wine (50ml);

- a standard pub measure of spirits (25ml).

The amount of alcohol varies in different types of drinks. Home brews can be stronger than bought, and home measures of spirits and wines tend to be more generous than pub measures.

9   Questions and answers

Question: *What is a healthy body weight?*

Answer: A healthy body weight is having a body mass index (BMI) between 20 and 25. BMI is calculated as:

$$BMI = \frac{body\ weight\ (kg)}{height\ (m)^2}$$

See chart on page 57.

Question: *How much fruit and vegetables is it recommended that we should be eating?*

Answer: At least five portions of fruit and vegetables a day are recommended.

A portion is:

- 2 tablespoonfuls of vegetables – raw, cooked, frozen or canned;
- 1 dessert bowlful of salad;
- 1 medium fruit, e.g. apple, banana, pear, orange;
- 2 small fruit, e.g. plum, small clementine, etc.;
- 1 cup of berries or grapes;
- 1 large slice of melon or pineapple;
- 2–3 tablespoonfuls of fresh fruit salad, stewed or canned fruit;
- 1 or more glasses (150ml) of fruit juice.

See pages 49 and 50 for a more extensive list.

Question: *How much dietary fibre is it recommended we aim to eat?*

Answer: In line with COMA's report on Dietary Reference Values[8], the average adult population intake of dietary fibre should increase from 12g a day to 18g. This applies to the majority of the adult population. See Table 4 on pages 51–2.

Question: *What is the evidence that red or processed meat is associated with cancer?*

Answer: There is evidence that the risk of developing colorectal cancer is significantly increased in high consumers of red and processed meat, and evidence for a number of mechanisms which might explain this. There is also evidence, though it is less strong, of an association between cancers of the breast, lung, prostate and pancreas and red and processed meat consumption.

Question: *Who needs to cut down on red or processed meat consumption?*

Answer: The recommendation applies to all adults who eat more than the current average of 90g cooked red and processed meat per day. It is especially applicable to the highest 15% of red and processed meat eaters, who regularly consume 140g cooked weight of red and processed meats per day. These tend to be men, and they also tend to be eating more food than the rest of the population. Few women need to cut down.

Question: **Will cutting down on red and processed meat consumption put some people at risk of iron deficiency anaemia?**

Answer: The recommendation to consider cutting down only applies to those adults who eat more than the current average of 90g cooked red and processed meat a day and especially to the highest consumers, who are mostly men. The recommendation does not apply to children or those adults, including most women, who eat less than 90g cooked red and processed meat a day. These are the groups most vulnerable to anaemia. Red meat is an important source of easily absorbed iron, and those who eat less than 90g a day should not reduce their intake.

Question: **Why are we told to use ß-carotene and high doses of single nutrient supplements with caution?**

Answer: Some studies have highlighted the lack of information on the long-term safety of sustained intakes of high doses of micronutrient supplements. Two recent large intervention trials set up to investigate the benefits of ß-carotene found that taking high doses of ß-carotene was more harmful than beneficial. Smokers who took the ß-carotene had a higher risk of lung cancer and heart disease compared with people who did not.

Question: **Why isn't there a recommendation on fat intake?**

Answer: Although there is some evidence which suggests there is a link between cancer and high fat intakes, the evidence was not strong or consistent enough to make a recommendation. However, this does not mean fat intakes should remain the same or rise. A reduction in fat intake, as recommended in previous COMA reports, is likely to contribute to a reduction in obesity.

Appendices

Glossary

ß-carotene	a form of vitamin A found in plants which the body can convert to vitamin A. It can act as an antioxidant
antioxidants	these protect against cell damage due to oxidation
Body Mass Index (BMI)	indirect measure of body fatness: $$\frac{\text{body weight (in kilograms)}}{\text{height (in metres) squared}}$$
carotenoids	group of pigments found in plants, many of which can act as antioxidants
case control study	matches people with a disease to those without disease and looks at the risk factors which each are exposed to
endometrium	lining of the womb or uterus
epidemiology	the study of disease within and between populations
flavonoids	compounds found in foods such as tea, plants, fruit and vegetables, which may act as antioxidants
heterocyclic amines	compounds which form on the surface of meat and other protein-containing foods when cooked. Some are carcinogenic in laboratory animals
incidence rate	the number of new cases of a disease registered in a population, usually expressed as cases per year per 100,000 of the population

intervention trial	a study which changes an aspect of the status of the subjects, and looks at the effect on disease
N-nitroso compounds	compounds formed from red meat which may cause cancer
non-starch polysaccharides	precise term for the major component of what is often called 'dietary fibre'
obesity	Body Mass Index (BMI) 30 or more
oestrogen	a hormone formed by the ovary, placenta, testes and possibly the adrenal cortex
phytoestrogens	oestrogen-like compounds found in some plants such as linseed and soya
pro-oxidant	encourage cell damage due to oxidation
prospective study	this starts by measuring the exposure of a group of people to a suspected risk factor, such as an element of the diet. The group of people (a cohort) is then studied over a period of time and the development of disease noted
relative risk	the ratio of the risk of an event among those exposed to a risk factor, to that of those unexposed
risk factor	any exposure or lifestyle factor which increases the risk of developing a given disease

References

1 Department of Health (1998) *Nutritional Aspects of the Development of Cancer*. Report on Health and Social Subjects No. 48. Stationery Office, London.

2 Department of Health (1995). *Sensible Drinking. The Report of an Inter-departmental Working Group*. Department of Health, London.

3 Committees on Toxicity, Mutagenicity, Carcinogenicity of Chemicals in Food, Consumer Products and the Environment (1996) *Annual Report 1995*. HMSO, London.

4 Parkin, D.M. *et al.* (1996) *Cancer Incidence in Five Continents Volume VI*. IARC Scientific Publications No. 120. International Agency for Research on Cancer, Lyon, France.

5 Doll, R. and Peto, R. (1981) 'The causes of cancer: quantitative estimates of avoidable risks of cancer in the United States today', *Journal of the National Cancer Institute*. vol. 66, 1191–308.

6 Willett, W. (1995) 'Diet, nutrition and avoidable cancer', *Environmental Health Perspectives*. vol. 103 (Supp. 8), 165–70.

7 Department of Health (1994) *Nutritional Aspects of Cardiovascular Disease*. Report on Health and Social Subjects No. 46. HMSO, London.

8 Department of Health (1991) *Dietary Reference Values for Food Energy and Nutrients for the United Kingdom*. Report on Health and Social Subjects No. 41. HMSO, London.

9 British Nutrition Foundation (1995) *Iron – Nutritional and Physiological Significance*. Chapman Hall, London.

10 Health Education Authority (1996) *Active for Life*. HEA, London.